多姿多彩、　　古色古香、
水乡画、　　　天堂周庄、

八四老人刘子蕃题

2001. 10. 4.

中国江南水乡

周　庄

周庄镇在中国的位置
Location of Zhouzhuang Town
周荘鎮の位置

北京 ★
Beijing

江苏
Jiangsu
周庄 上海
Zhouzhuang Shanghai

ZHOUZHUANG

A TOWNSHIP ON WATER IN SOUTHERN CHINA

中国旅游出版社
China Travel & Tourism Press

顾　问：庄春地

责任编辑：吕大千

中文撰稿：周锦骝

翻　译：王庆华(英文)　施殿文(日文)

图片编辑：刘大健　周仁德

绘　图：付　丽

装帧设计：董　刚

摄　影：(按姓氏笔划顺序)

刘大健　刘伟　任强　张尧俊　陈泳

张国香　沈绮湘　周仁德　金寿彭　杨振一

赵小军　晓庄　耿荣兴　常振国　董瑞成

图书在版编目(CIP)数据

周庄／刘大健等编. －北京：中国旅游出版社，
2001.1
　（旅游在中国. 中国江南水乡）
　ISBN 7-5032-1795-2

　Ⅰ.周... Ⅱ.刘... Ⅲ.旅游指南－周庄－画册
　Ⅳ. K928. 953. 5-64

中国版本图书馆CIP数据核字（2000）第82812号

中国旅游出版社出版发行
(北京建国门内大街甲九号)
东莞新扬印刷有限公司印刷
2001年1月第三版第六次印刷
开本：850×1168毫米　1/48
印数：38400-53400　　002800

古镇周庄

昆山市周庄镇位于苏州城东南 30 多公里处，旧名贞丰里，地处青浦、吴江、吴县、昆山四市县交界处。这里在春秋战国时期是吴王少子摇和汉越摇君的封地，始称摇城。北宋元祐元年（1086 年），周迪功郎信奉佛教，将庄田 13 公顷捐给全福寺作为庙产。后人为纪念周迪功郎，遂将贞丰里改名为周庄。

周庄，环境幽雅，建筑古朴，虽历经 900 多年沧桑，仍完整地保存着原来的水乡集镇的建筑格局。全镇百分之六十以上的民居仍为明清建筑，仅有 0.4 平方公里的小镇有近 100 座古典宅院和 60 多个砖雕门楼。如元末明初巨贾沈万三后裔所建的沈厅、明初中山王徐达后裔所建的张厅，都是明清住宅的典型。

周庄四面环水，犹如浮在水上的一朵睡莲。南北市河、后巷河、油车漾河、中市河，形成"井"字形，因河成街，傍水筑屋。有河有街必有桥。周庄桥多，是其特色之一。河是路的一种，桥是路的延续。小桥流水人家，优美幽谧和谐。这里有富安桥、贞丰桥、福洪桥、通秀桥、普庆桥、蚬园桥、梯云桥、报恩桥、隆兴桥、永安桥、世德桥、全功桥、青龙桥、蚬江桥、聚宝桥等等。特别有名的是永安桥和世德桥，又称双桥，由一座石拱桥和一座石梁桥组成，两条河水在这里交汇成"十"字，河上面石桥联袂而筑，桥面一横一竖，桥洞一方一圆，十分别致。坐在船上游览，穿桥过洞，颇有情趣。每穿过一个桥洞就出现一种景色；每拐过一座桥堍，又另有一种意境，从不同角度构成一幅美妙的"小桥、流水、人家"的水乡风情画。待到夜幕降临，店铺上好门板，人去街空，街上一片寂静，狭窄的巷道，昏黄的街灯，在您面前是万籁俱静的小镇。这时，您在河边慢步，走过小街，穿过小桥，或凝视宁静水面，或仰看天际点点繁星，或倾听屋里传出来的隐隐的欢声笑语，您可任意冥思遐想，尽情享受小镇的宁静、和谐、温馨、淡泊的动人风情！

周庄的魅力，还在于它的文化蕴涵。沈厅、张厅、迷楼、叶楚伧故居、澄虚道院、全福寺等名胜古迹，具有一定的历史、文化和观赏价值。西晋文学家张翰（字季鹰），唐代诗人刘禹锡、陆龟蒙等曾寓居周庄；元末明初沈万三得天时地利，成为江南巨富；近代柳亚子、陈去病等南社发起人，曾聚会迷楼饮酒吟诗；当代名人到周庄采风者更不胜枚举，像台湾作家三毛那样钟情周庄，像旅美华人画家陈逸飞画了油画《双桥》后和"双桥"一样驰名世界，像著名古画家吴冠中赞誉"周庄集中国水乡之美"，像著名建筑学家罗哲文的称颂"周庄是中国的一个宝"等等，他们对周庄情由独钟，可见周庄的魅力何其无穷！

Zhouzhuang, an Ancient Town

Zhouzhuang Town, once called Zhenfengli, is located in Kunshan City, 30 km to the southeast of Suzhou in Jiangsu Province covering an area of 0.4 sq. km. Apart from Kunshan, it is also closely linked with Qingpu, Wujiang and Wuxian County.

The above four places were called Yaocheng in ancient times and were the fief in the Spring and Autumn Period (770-476 B.C.). In 1086, Zhou Digong, a noted Buddhist, contributed 13 hectares of land to the Quanfu Temple (Full Fortune), which later took the name of Zhouzhuang Town as a memorial to Zhou.

Zhouzhuang is well known for its beautiful environment and simple architecture. Although more than 900 years have past, its architectural style is still well preserved. More than 60 percent of the residential houses were built during the Ming (1368-1644) and Qing (1644-1911) dynasties, consisting of nearly 100 classic courtyards and 60 carved brick archways.

Like a lotus on the water, the town is surrounded and bisected by rivers including Nanbeichi, Houxiang, Youcheyang and Zhongshi. There are many bridges as well, including Fu'an, Zhenfeng, Fuhong, Tongxiu, Puqing, Xianyuan, Tiyun, Bao'en, Longxing, Yong'an, Shide, Quangong, Qinglong, Xianhong and Jubao, the most famous being Yong'an and Shide, known as Double Bridge, one a stone arch type and the other a stone beam type bridge.

Two rivers crisscross in north-south and east-west directions here, and the square and round openings of the bridges provide a unique frame for the water scenery.

Sitting on the boat, one may enjoying the scene between bridges and feel the interest of a water township which offers a quiet and simple life. When night falls, all streets are empty. Down the narrow lanes one catches a glimpse of dim lights. Walking by the waterside, along the road or over a bridge, the peace of the calm water and clear sky, perhaps punctuated occasionally by the distant sound of laughter, creates a harmonious and sweet environment.

The town has many cultural relics, including the houses of Shen and Zhang, the Milou Tower, Ye Chucang's Former Residence, Chengxu Taoist Temple and Quanfu Temple.

Many ancient and modern scholars have lived in or visited the town, such as ancient Zhang Han, a literati of the Western Jin Dynasty (265-317), Liu Yuxi and Lu Guimeng, two poets of the Tang Dynasty (618-907), as well as modern Sanmao, a noted woman writer from Taiwan, and artist Chen Yifei. Chen's painting, "The Double Bridge", is as famous as the real double bridge in the town. A well-known Chinese artist Wu Guanzhong once praised the town as a collection of beauty of China's water townships. Luo Zhewen, a notable architect, described Zhouzhuang as "a treasure of China".

古い町——周荘

昆山市周荘鎮は蘇州市の南東30余キロのところに

あり、旧名は貞豊里といわれ、青浦、呉江、呉県、昆山の4市県の境が接したところにある。春秋戦国時代は呉王の少子揺と漢の越揺君の領地で、揺城といわれていた。北宋の元祐元年（1086）仏教を信奉していた周迪功郎が13ヘクタールの農地を寄付して全福寺を建てた。後世の人は周迪功郎を記念するため、貞豊里を周荘と改称した。

周荘は環境が幽静、建築が古朴で、900年以上の歴史を有しているが、今でも昔からの水郷の建築がよく保存されている。町全体の60%以上の民家はやはり明・清時代の建てられたもので、わずか0.4平方キロの小さな町に約100ヵ所の古い邸宅と60余りの磚彫門楼（煉瓦造りの彫刻の施された屋根つきの門）がある。例えば、元末・明初の大商人であった沈万三の後裔の建てた沈庁、明初の中山王の徐達の後裔の建てた張庁はいずれも明・清時代の邸宅の典型である。

周荘の周りは水に囲まれ、まるで水面に浮かぶスイレンのようである。南北市河、后巷河、油車漾河、中市河は「井」の字形を呈し、川に沿って街が造られ、民家が建てられている。川があり街があると必ず橋がある。橋が多いのが周荘の特色の一つとなっている。川が道であり、橋は道の延長である。小さな橋，流れる川、素朴な民家が調和のとれた美しさをかもし出している。ここには富安橋、貞豊橋、福洪橋、通秀橋、普慶橋、`蜆園橋、梯雲橋、報恩橋、隆興橋、永安橋、世徳橋、全功橋、青竜橋、蜆江橋、聚宝橋などの橋がある。なかでも有名なのは永安橋と世徳橋で、双橋ともいわれ、石造りのアーチ橋と石造りの梁橋からなっている。二本の川がここで合流して「十」字形を呈し、二つの石橋が連なって架けられ、橋面は一方は横に、もう一方は縦に走り、橋の孔は一方が方形、もう一方が円形で、非常にユニークである。舟に乗って、橋の下を通ると、とても情趣がある。橋の下を通るごとに、一つの景色が現れ、橋のたもとを曲がるごとに、もう一つの境地が現れ、異なる角度から「小さな橋、流れる川、素朴な民家」が織りなす美しい水郷の風情画を構築している。夜のとばりが下りると、店は閉められ、人は家に帰り、街は人影もなく、ひっそりし、狭い路地に街灯がともし、街全体が静寂になる。この時、川のほとりをゆっくり歩き、狭い道を通り、小さな橋を渡ったり、静かな水面に目をやったり、夜空の無数の星を仰いだり、家屋から伝わって来るなごやかな笑い声を耳にしたりして、思いをはせると、小さな町の静かな、平和な、温かい、淡白な感動的な風情を享受することができる。

周荘の魅力はまたその文化の内容にある。沈庁、張庁、迷楼、葉楚傖旧居、澄虚道院、全福寺などの名所旧跡は、一定の歴史的、文化的な観賞価値がある。西晋の文学者張翰（字を季鷹という）、唐代の詩人劉禹錫、陸亀蒙らは周荘に住んでいた。元末・明初の沈万三は天の時、地の利を生かして江南の富豪となった。近代の柳亜子、陳去病らの南社の発起人はかつて迷楼に集まって酒を飲んだり、詩を作ったりした。現代でも多くの人が周荘を訪れている。台湾の作家三毛は周荘をこよなく愛し、中国系アメリカ人の画家陳逸飛は油絵「双橋」を描き、世界的に有名になり、著名な古画家呉冠中は「周荘は中国の水郷の美を集めている」と称え、著名な建築家羅哲文は「周荘は中国の宝である」と称賛し、みな周荘に深い感情をもっている。これからも分かるように、周荘は魅力にあふれる水郷である。

周庄镇略图
Map of Zhouzhuang Town
周莊鎮略図

往昆山、苏州
To Kunshan、
Suzhou

镇政府
Town Government

往上海
To Shanghai

高尔夫球场
Golf Course
ゴルフ場

白蚬湖
Baixian Lake

北 白 荡
Bei Baidang

周庄大桥
Zhouzhuang Grand Bridge

申江大酒店
Shenjiang Hotel

旅游公司
Tourism Co.

邮电局
Post Office

汽车站
Bus Station
バス停留所

天天江酒店
Tian Tianhui
Wineshop

周庄医院 ✚
Zhouzhuang Hospital
周庄医院

周庄旅行社
Zhouzhuang Travel Service

光工路
Quangong Road

全福塔
Quanfu Tower

中房宾馆
Zhongfang Hotel

沈万三水底墓
Shen Wansan
Water Tomb

南湖旅游
度假区
Nanhu Tourism
Holiday Area

贞丰泽国古牌楼
Zhenfeng Zeguo Pailou
真豐沢国の古牌楼

古镇照壁
Ancient Screen Wall
古鎮の照壁（目隠しの壁）

NAM
张厅
Zhang Hall

澄虚道院
Chengxu Taoist Temple

迷楼
Mi Building

叶楚伧故居
Ye Chulun
Formal Residence

沈厅
Shen Hall

全福寺
Quan Fu Temple

南 湖
Nanhu Lake

江南水乡
A township on water in Southern China
江南の水郷

古镇周庄
Zhouzhuang, an ancient town
古い町——周荘

双桥(钥匙桥)
Double Bridge (Key Bridge)
双橋(かぎ橋)

中市河
Zhongshi River
中市河

古民居沈厅
Shen's House
古い民居——沈庁

松茂堂

沈厅安乐所
Anle Hall in Shen's House
沈庁の安楽所

明清建筑

沈厅 位于周庄富安桥东垸南侧南市街上,由沈万三后裔沈本仁于清乾隆七年(1742年)所建。七进五门楼,大小100间房屋,分布在100米长的中轴线两侧,占地2000多平方米。

沈厅,由三部分组成。前部是水墙门、河埠,供家人停靠船只、洗涤衣物之用;中部是墙门楼、茶厅、正厅,为接送宾客,办理婚丧大事及议事之处;后部是大堂楼、小堂楼、后厅屋,为生活起居之所。整个厅堂是典型的"前厅后堂"的建筑格局。前后

屋之间均由过街楼和过道阁所连接。正厅堂是"松茂堂",占地170平方米。朝正堂的砖雕门楼,是五个门楼中最雄伟的一个,高达6米,正中有匾额"积厚流光",四周为"红梅迎春"浮雕,所雕人物、走兽及亭台楼阁、戏文故事等,栩栩如生,非常传神。

Architecture of Ming and Qing

Shen's House Shen's House is located to the southeast of Fu'an Bridge, on Nanshi Street. It was built in 1742 during the Qing Dynasty by Shen Benren, a descendant of Shen Wansan who was a man of wealth in southern China during late Yuan (1206-1368) to early Ming dynasties.

It consists of seven courtyards, five archways, more than 100 rooms of different sizes along two sides of a 100-m-long axis road, covering an area of 2,000 sq. m., offering a unique traditional Chinese architectural style.

It has three sections. The first includes the water gate and wharf for mooring boats and for washing. The second one consists of the Tea Hall and Main Hall for receiving guests and holding wedding or funeral ceremonies. The rear part serves as living quarters.

The Main Hall covers 170 sq. m. The six-m-high carved brick archway, facing the Main Hall, is the most magnificent among the five, with a horizontal inscribed board bearing the inscrip-

tion, Jihouliuguang (do more good for ever).
Around the board are relief sculptures of fig-
urines, animals, pavilions and opera characters.

明・清時代の建築

沈庁　周荘富安橋東のたもとの南側の南市街にあり、沈万三の後裔である沈本仁が清の乾隆7年 (1742) に建てたもので、7庭5門からなり、大小の部屋が100間あり、長さ100メートルの中軸線の両側に並び、敷地面積は約2000平方メートル。

　沈庁は三つの部分からなる。前部は水墙門、河埠があり、船を停めたり、洗濯することに使われた。中部は墙門楼、茶室、広間があり、客様を送迎したり、婚礼・葬儀を行ったり、会合を行ったりするところで

あった。後部は大堂楼、小堂楼、后庁屋があり、日常生活をするところであった。全体は典型的な「前庁後堂」（前部は広間、後部は居間）の配置になっている。前後の建物は過街楼、過道閣でつながっている。正堂の「松茂堂」は敷地面積が170平方メートル。その前にある磚彫門楼は五つの門楼の中の最も大きく、高さは6メートルあり、その正面に「積厚流光」という扁額がかかっており、周りは「紅梅迎春」の浮き彫りで、人物、動物および亭・台・楼・閣、物語などは生き生きとしている。

跑马楼
Paoma Tower
跑馬楼

沈厅中轴线
Axis of the Shen's House
沈厅の中軸線

沈厅前厅
Front Hall of the Shen's House
沈厅の前庁

沈厅"松茂堂"
Songmao Hall of the Shen's House
沈厅「松茂堂」

小院
Small courtyard
小さな庭

翠竹
Bamboo
竹

21

沈厅绣楼
Embroidery Room of the Shen's House
沈庁の女子の居室

绣娘(腊塑)
Wax statue of an embroider lady
刺繍をしている娘(ろう像)

沈厅酒楼
Restaurant in Shen's House
沈庁のレストラン

临河茶室
Teahouse by river
川に面する茶室

张厅　位于北市街双桥之南,原名怡顺堂,为明代中山王徐达之弟徐逵后裔于明正统年间(1436－1449年)所建,清初转让张姓,改为玉燕堂,俗称张厅。

　　张厅前后六进,房屋70余间,占地1800多平方米。进门两侧是厢房楼,楼下楼上设蠡壳长短窗,显得古朴典雅。玉燕堂为主厅,轩敞明亮,古雅朴实,粗大的厅柱挺立在楠木鼓墩上,坚固如石,实为明代住宅遗风,较为罕见。厅旁有一条小河穿屋而过,河水中段设一丈余见方的水池,供船只交会和调头用。驳岸拥围,缆石各异,扁舟临岸,一派"船从家中过"的情景。后厅临河设一排敞窗,窗前设吴王靠,又叫美人靠,透过窗户可赏后院花草树木,咫尺千里,余味无穷。张厅为江苏省重点文物保护单位。

Zhang's House　Zhang's House is located at the south of the Double Bridge on Beishi Street. Built between 1436 and 1449 by the offspring of Xu Kui, the brother of Zhongshan King Xu Da, it was sold to the Zhang's Family during the early Qing Dynasty, after which it was called either Yuyan (Jade Swallow) Hall or Zhang's House.

　　It has six courtyards and more than 70 rooms, covering more than 1,800 sq. m. The first courtyard has side buildings on the east and west, with long and short windows. Yuyan Hall is the main building, large and bright with grand columns on big *nanmu* pier bases, a rare Ming style. A river flows by the hall, with a square pool built in the middle section to allow boats to turn round. Its rear hall has open windows and balconies facing the water with a backyard of various plants and flowers.

The place now is an important cultural relic under provincial protection.

張庁　北市街の双橋の南にあり、原名は怡順堂といわれ、明代の中山王徐達の弟である徐達の後裔が明の正統年間（1436〜1449）に建てたもので、清初に張姓に譲渡し、玉燕堂と改称された。俗称は張庁という。

張庁は6庭があり、部屋は70余間、敷地面積は1800余メートル。入口の門を入ると、両側に廂房楼（母屋の両わきに向かい合った棟）があり、各階に貝殻で飾った大小の窓がついており、古朴、典雅である。玉燕堂はメーン・ホールで、広くて明るく、古雅、素朴で、太い柱が楠の台座にしっかり立っている。これは明代の住宅の遺風で、たいへん珍しい。庁の傍に小川があって部屋の下を流れ、川の中段に3.3メートルほどの四角い池があり、船の向きを変えるのに用いられる。岸にある繋舟柱はいろいろな石で作られている。「舟は家の中を通る」ようになっている。後庁は川に面して多くの窓がつけられ、窓の前に美人靠ともいわれる呉王靠（もたれのある椅子）が置かれてあり、窓越しに裏庭の花草樹木を観賞でき、近くにあって広さを感じさせ、言外の趣がある。張庁は江蘇省の重点保護文化財に指定されている。

雕花門楼
Carved archway
花彫りの門楼

张厅"玉燕堂"
Yuyan Hall in Zhang's House
張庁「玉燕堂」

船从家中过
Boat passing through house
家を通る舟

小商店
Grocery store
小売店

通往银子浜的小河
A River to the river Yinzibang
銀子浜に流れる小川

临水人家
A residential house at the bank
川に面する民家

南湖帆影
South Lake scenery
南湖の帆影

有望湖楼、湖心亭、九曲桥,凌波石舫隔水相望;池边垂柳依依,百花争艳,夏日翠荷玉立,金鲤跃波,富有诗情画意。秋景区集厅、堂、轩、祠、榭、廊、亭、假山于一园,并建有思鲈堂、季鹰斋、刘宾客舍和梦得榭。冬景区以全福寺为中心,有"水中佛国"之称。

Scenic Spots

South Lake South Lake, also known as Nanbaidang, is located in the south of the town and is under the jurisdiction of both Zhouzhuang and Wujiang City. By the lakeshore, tourists may visit dense bamboo forests and enjoy clear water in the quiet environment. Local people made use of the natural scenery and historical relics of the lake and constructed the South Lake Garden.

The garden, consisting of the four scenic areas of Spring, Summer, Autumn and Winter, covers 3.6 hectares. The Lotus Pond is the center of the Spring and Autumn scenic areas with Viewing Lake Tower, Mid-Lake Pavilion, Bridge of Nine Turnings, and Riding-Wave Marble Boat around. The combination of willows, flowers and fish, provides a beautiful environment. Its Autumn Area has various halls, pavilions, corridors and rockeries. And the Winter area centers on the Quanfu Temple.

风光名胜

南湖 位于周庄镇南面,俗称南白荡,现统称南湖。南湖的三分之一面积属周庄;其余属吴江市。湖滨茂林修竹,环境雅静;湖光水色,清幽透明,是游人的好去处。人们又充分利用南湖自然风光及历史胜迹,创建了南湖园。全园分春、夏、秋、冬四个景区,占地3.6公顷,建筑面积6300平方米。春夏景区为山水园林,以荷花池为中心,临池而建的

名　所

南湖　周荘鎮の南にあり、俗称は南白蕩といい、今は南湖といわれている。南湖の3分の1は周荘に属し、残りは呉江市に属している。湖のほとりには樹木、竹が茂り、静かである。湖の景色が美しく、訪れる人が多い。南湖園は南湖の自然風光および歴史的名所が十分に生かされている。春、夏、秋、冬の四つの風景区にからなり、敷地面積は3.6ヘクタール、建築面積は6300平方メートル。春夏風景区は山水庭園で、荷花池を中心とし、望湖楼、湖心亭、九曲橋などがあり、凌波石舫は水を隔てて目と鼻の先にある。池のほとりには垂れ柳が揺れ、花が咲き、夏は緑の蓮の花がきれいに咲き、鯉が泳ぎ、詩情と画境に富んでいる。秋風景区は庁、堂、軒、祠、水際の亭、廊下、亭、築山などがあり、思鱸堂、季鷹斎、劉賓客舎、夢得榭が建てられている。冬風景区は全福寺を中心としており、「水中の仏の国」といわれている。

南湖度假村
South Lake Holiday Resort
南湖リゾート

南湖落日
Setting sun in the South Lake
南湖の夕陽

南湖鹅戏
White Geese in the South Lake
南湖で楽しむガチョウ

Quanfu Teaching Temple　Established by Zhou Digong in 1086, it is located on the bank of the Baixian Lake. The temple has been expanded in the successive dynasties and is well known in the region.

In the 1950s, it was changed into a grain depot, then all the Buddhist statues and collected treasures were destroyed.

The temple was rebuilt in March 1995, and the construction completed within one year.

It combined Buddhist culture with architechtural arts, offering beautiful environment and unique scenery.

The building posseses yellow walls and black tiles, caved beams and painted rafters. Main buildings include the Temple Gate, Zhigui Pavilion, Hall of Mahatma and Buddhist Sutra Tower.

全福讲寺　北宋元祐元年（1086 年），里人周迪功郎，舍宅建寺，名全福讲寺，位于白蚬湖畔。后经历代扩建，梵宫重叠，香火旺盛，成为远近闻名的寺院。到了本世纪五十年代，殿宇改作粮库，所有佛像和寺藏珍品也毁于一旦。在改革的春风中，周庄镇为发展旅游业，于 1995 年 3 月 18 日破土重建全福讲寺。历时不到一年，一座全新的寺庙建成了。主要建筑有：山门、指归阁、大雄宝殿、藏经楼等。整座寺庙结构严整，殿宇轩昂，黄墙黛瓦，雕梁画栋，蔚为大观。借水布景，巧夺天工，楼阁殿宇，鳞次栉比。既有佛教文化的博大精深，又有建筑艺术的美轮美奂，园林景色，如诗如画，令游人流连忘返。

全福講寺　白蜆湖のほとりにある。北宋の元祐元年（1086）に周迪功郎が建てたものである。その後いくたび拡張されて、お参りする人が多くなり、遠近に名が知られるようになった。今世紀の 50 年代に、建物が穀物倉庫に変わり、仏像と寺内の珍品が破壊された。改革の中で、周荘鎮は観光業を発展させるため、1995年 3 月 18 日から全福講寺を再建し、一年足らずで新しい寺院が完成した。主な建築は山門、指帰閣、大雄宝殿、蔵経楼（経書収蔵楼）などからなる。寺院の構造は整然とし、仏閣が高く、壁は黄色で瓦は青黒色で、

彫刻が施され、壮観である。水景色を巧みに生かして、
楼閣・仏閣が建てられている。仏教文化の神髄、建築
芸術の美が融合し、景色が詩や絵のように、美しく、
多くの観光客を引き付けている。

全福讲寺
Quanfu jiang Temple
全福講寺

水中佛国
Buddhist Area on Water
水中の仏の国

全福塔　是一座集观赏与实用于一身的仿古造型的水塔。建于 1987 年，共 5 层，高 33 米。塔内有楼梯达顶，可观览古镇全景。与"贞丰泽国"石牌楼对峙而立在同一视线里，成为周庄镇标志性建筑。

Quanfu Pagoda　Quanfu Pagoda is a imitation of an ancient-style pagoda actually built in 1987. It has five floors, and is 33 meters high, offering a panorama view of the whole town, serving as the symbol of Zhouzhuang.

全福塔　観賞と実用を一つにした古風な水塔である。1987 年に建てられ、5 層からなり、高さは 33 メートル。塔内の梯子を登って頂部に立つと、周荘の全景が眺められる。「貞豊沢国」石牌楼と対峙して立ち、周荘鎮のシンボル的建築となっている。

节日的全福塔
Festival at Quanfu Pagoda
祝祭日の全福塔

贞丰牌楼
Zhenfeng Archway
貞豊の牌楼

澄虚道院
Chengxu Taoist Temple
澄虚道院

澄虚道院　　位于中市街上,面对普庆桥,俗称"圣堂",建于北宋元祐年间(1086－1093年),距今已有900多年的历史。自明代中叶以后,道院规模日趋恢宏,清乾隆时,已形成前后三进的宏大建筑,占地1500平方米,为吴中地区知名道院之一。院内主要建筑有玉皇阁、文昌阁、圣帝阁等。玉皇阁为正殿,建于宋代。

　　Chengxu Taoist Temple　　Chengxu Taoist Temple, also known as Shentang Hall, is located on Zhongshi Street, facing the Puqing Bridge. It was built between 1086-1093. Since the mid-Ming Dynasty, the temple has taken shape, and in the Qing Dynasty, it was expanded to three big courtyards, covering 1, 500 sq. m., serving as one of the four notable Taoist temples in Wuzhong Region. Its main buildings are Yuhuang, Wenchang and Shengdi pavilions. The Yuhuang Pavilion was built in the Song Dynasty.

　　澄虚道院　　中市街にあり、向かいに普慶橋である。「聖堂」ともいわれ、北宋の元祐年間(1086～1093)に建てられ、900年余りの歴史をもっている。明代の中葉から、規模が拡大され、清の乾隆時代には三つの庭のある建築群となり、敷地面積は1500平方メートルで、呉中地区の有名な道院の一つである。院内の主な建築は玉皇閣、文昌閣、聖帝閣などがある。玉皇閣は正殿で、宋代に建てられた。

学一着
Learn to play
一業を学ぶ
周庄棋苑
Chess House of Zhouzhuang
周荘の将棋室

白蚬湖 位于周庄镇西侧,它是一条长约 5 公里水道,俗称白蚬江,因江中盛产白蚬而得名。面积 7.6 平方千米,平均水深 2.5 米。每晚渔船归来,在江畔抛锚泊船,晾网卖鱼,唱起小曲,一派"渔舟唱晚"的情调。

Baixian Lake Baixian Lake, west of the town, is a 5-km-long water route with an average depth of 2.5 m, covering an area of 7.6 sq. m. Every evening, boats and fishermen come back to sell their catch, their shouts mingling with the songs that can be heard far and wide.

白蚬湖
Baixian Lake
白蚬湖

白蜆湖 周荘鎮の西側にある長さ5キロの川で、白蜆江ともいわれ、白蜆が多くとれれることからこの名がある。面積は7600平方メートルで、平均水深は2.5メートル。毎晩漁舟が戻ると、漁民たちは漁網を干し、魚を売り、小唄を歌い、「漁舟晩唱う」の情調にあふれる。

春汛
Spring flood
春の漁

白蚬湖落日
Sunset at Baixian Lake
白蜆湖の夕日

水巷古桥
Ancient bridge
水巷の古い橋

水巷风光　走进周庄,漫步在岸边的石板小路上,或乘摇橹小舟荡漾在碧波盈盈的小河里,穿过一座一座石拱桥,看两岸纯朴民风,十分有趣。两岸民房,多为二层楼,粉墙黛瓦,木棂花窗。经常可以看到一根根晾衣竹竿从窗户伸出来搭在另一间房屋的瓦上,或从屋檐上吊下的竹钩上,挑起五颜六色的衣服。时而有一只吊桶从上面"卟通"入水,拎上来满桶清水,用其拖地或洗涤。更多的人习惯把菜和米,甚至吃过饭的锅和碗都拿到河边清洗。小船把鱼虾蔬菜运到河边,泊在桥洞旁,楼上人便用绳子吊下竹篮与之交易。沿河驳岸上,嵌有形态各异的缆船石,每隔 10 米就有一块,有如意状,有怪兽状,有牛鼻朝天,有鲤鱼腾跃,造型生动古朴。

Water Route　The most interesting travel route is walking along the banks or rowing a boat through the stone arch bridges to view the residential houses along the waterside. The houses commonly have two floors, with white walls and black roofs, various styles of windows out of which often poke many bamboo poles carrying the household laundry. The local people use the water to do their washing, and also do their shopping by lowering a pole with a basket on the end to the vendors sitting in their boats. Along the roads, there are various forms of stone blocks every 10 meters for the boats stop.

水巷風光　周荘の岸辺の石畳道を散策したり、小舟に乗って多くの石橋を通り、両岸の素朴な風情を見るのも楽しい。両岸の民家の多くは2階建てで、壁は白く瓦は青黒色で、模様入りの木窓がついている。窓から伸び出してもう一つの部屋の瓦の上にかけられた干し竿や、ひさしから吊るされた竹の鉤に、色とりどりの衣服がかかっている。桶を川に下ろし水を汲み上げたりしている光景も時折り見かける。多くの人々は習慣的に野菜や米、さらに鍋や茶碗を川辺で洗っている。魚、エビや野菜をのせた舟が川辺や橋の傍に停まり、二階から縄で下ろされる竹籠にこれらを入れて売っている。川岸には、いろいろな形をした繋船石が10メートル置きに立っており、如意形、怪獣形、天に向けた牛の鼻の形、飛び上がる鯉形など造型が生き生きとして素朴である。

船娘
Woman boater
舟を漕ぐ娘

水巷
Water route in the village
水巷

中市河
Zhongshi River
中市河

穿竹石栏
Stone fence through bamboo
竹と石の欄干

水路弯弯
Winding water route
曲りくねた水路

波光船影
Boats on the River
浪と船の影

看风情游周庄
Experience Zhouzhuang on boat
周荘を見物

晨雾
Fog in dawn
朝の霧

后港人家
Residential houses
at Rear Port
後港の民家

古镇石板路
Stone road
古い町の石畳道

中市街
Zhongshi Street
中市街

小巷
Narrow Lane
小さな路地
水乡暮色
Water township in dusk
水郷の夕暮れの景色

故乡的桥
Hometown Bridge
故郷の橋

双桥 由世德桥和永安桥纵横相接,石阶相连,组成双桥,位于镇东北部,建于明万历年间(1573－1619年)。银子浜和南北市河在此交汇成十字。聪明的工匠在此联袂建造两座石桥,桥面一横一竖,桥洞一方一圆,样子很像古代的钥匙,所以人们又称之为钥匙桥。1984年,旅美上海青年画家陈逸飞,以双桥为题材,创作了一幅题为《故乡的回忆》油画,连同其他37幅油画在美国西方石油公司董事长阿曼德·哈默的画廊展出,后又被哈默购下,作为礼物送给邓小平,以双桥象征中美两国人民的友谊、合作与和平。1985年,这幅油画又被印上当

年联合国首日封,让世界上越来越多的人领略了周庄古镇秀美的风光,古朴的风韵。双桥,不似钥匙,胜似钥匙。这把友好的钥匙开启了国际交往的友好之门。

Double Bridge Double Bridge, built between 1513 and 1619, consists of the Shide and Yong'an bridges and is situated to the northeast of the town.

The area is crossed by the Yinzi and Nanbei rivers, and the bridges are built in one in the direction of north-south and the other east-west, with one square and one round openings. Because they look like an ancient key, it also known as Key Bridge.

Chen Yifei, a young artist residing in the U.S., created a picture of "Memories of Hometown" based on the Double Bridge in 1984. The painting, with Chen's other 37 works, were exhibited and bought by Dr. Armond Hammer, an American oil tycoon, and later presented to the late Deng Xiaoping. The painting symbolizes the friendship, cooperation and peace between the two countries. In 1985, the painting was used on a first day cover issued by the UN, so that more and more people came to know of Zhouzhuang's beautiful scenery.

双橋 世徳橋と永安橋が縦横に石段でつながっているので、双橋といわれている。町の北東部にあり、明代の万歴年間(1573～1619)に建てられた銀子浜と

南北市河がここで合流して十字形を呈し、その上に連接した二つの石橋が架けられている。橋面は一方が横に、もう一方が縦に走り、橋の孔は一方が方形、もう一方が円形で、古代の鍵のような形状をしているから鑰匙橋ともいわれる。1984年、アメリカ留学の上海青年画家陳逸飛が、双橋を題材とした「故郷の思い出」を創作し、その他の37点の油絵と一緒にアメリカのオクシデンタル石油会社会長のアーマンド・ハマー氏のギャリラーに展示され、その後ハマー氏がこれを買い、中米両国人民の友情、協力と平和のシンボルとして鄧小平氏に贈った。1985年、この油絵はまたその年の国連の初日カバーの切手に印刷され、世界の多くの人が周荘の美しい風光、古朴風情に触れる機会を得た。双橋は鍵の形に似ているが、鍵より勝っている。この鍵は国際交流の友好の門を開けた。

古鎮晨曦
Dawn in town
古い町の朝

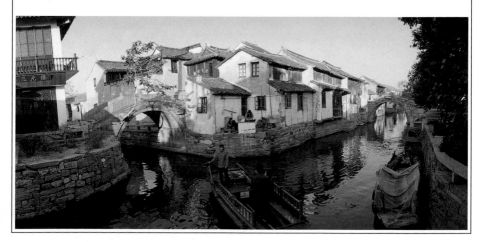

双桥
Double Bridge
双橋

太平桥
Taiping Bridge
太平橋

古镇
Sunset
古い町

历经风雨
A bridge inscribed with
changes of ages
蔵月を経った橋と民家

古桥石雕
Carved Stone Bridge
古い橋の石彫り

三元楼
Sanyuan Restaurant
三元楼

永安雪霁
Yong'an Bridge after snow
永安の雪の晴れ

清晨古镇
Early morning of the town
朝の古い町

富安桥 位于周庄中市街东端,横跨南北市河,通南北市街,是古镇桥与楼联袂结构完美的独特建筑。桥身四侧的桥楼临波拔起,遥遥相对,气势非凡,为江南水乡仅存的立体型桥楼合壁建筑。始建于元至正十五年(1355年),后由沈万三之弟沈万四出资重建,成石拱桥,改名富安桥,期望既富又安,心诚可见,后人永不忘怀。现在四侧桥楼保存完好,飞檐朱栏,雕梁画栋,古色古香,楼内设茶室、餐馆和商店,游人既可歇憩,又可赏景,别有情趣。

Fu'an Bridge Fu'an Bridge is located at the east end of Zhongshi Street, crossing the Nanbeishi River and leading to the Nanbeishi Street.

It was built in 1355, and rebuilt by Shen Wansi, younger brother of Shen Wansan. It has towers on all four corners. Each side has carved beams and painted rafters. People can now enjoy local foods and shopping in the towers.

富安橋 周荘中市街の東端にあり、南北市河に架けられ、南北市街に通じており、橋と楼(建物)からなる独特な構築物である。橋の四側に楼が建てられ、互いに相対し、壮観である。江南水郷のわずかしか保存されていない橋と楼が一体になった立体建築である。元代の至正15年(1355)、その後沈万三の弟である沈万四が出資して再建し、アーチ型の石橋となり、富安橋と改称された。富裕、安定の意味がこめられており、その期待を後世の人はいつまでも忘れていない。現在、四側の橋と楼はよく保存されており、軒先がそり返り、欄干が赤く、彫刻などが施され、古めかしく優雅で、楼内には茶室、レストラン、商店があり、観光客は休憩することもできれば、景色を観賞することもできる。

游船码头
Boat wharf
観光舟のふ頭

一日游
One – Day Tour
一日コース

富安茶楼
Fu'an Teahouse
富安茶楼

富安桥
Fu'an Bridge
富安橋

桥头
Bridge end
橋のたもと

贞丰桥
Zhenfeng Bridge
貞豊橋

贞丰桥 位于中市河西口,连接贞丰弄和西湾街,因周庄古名贞丰里而得名。明、清时皆有重修,风貌如初,仍傲然跨河而立。桥北西侧,曾开设德记酒店,地处桥旁与闹市中间,顾客把酒临风,看窗外波光桥影,舟楫往来,桥楼互衬,风情无限,美不胜收。

Zhenfeng Bridge Zhenfeng Bridge is sitting on the west mouth of Zhongshi River, and connects the Zhenfeng Lane and Xiwan Street. It was rebuilt in Ming and Qing dynasties, and is well-preserved today.

貞豊橋 中市河の西口にあり、貞豊弄と西湾街を結び、周荘の旧名をとってこの名がある。明・清の時代にもと通りに修復された。橋の北西側に徳記酒店がある。橋の傍と賑やかな市街区の中間にあり、客は酒を飲みながら、外の景色、船の往来を眺めることができ、橋と楼が互いに映え合った風情に趣があり、美しい。

青龙桥
Qinglong Bridge
青竜橋

二龙石雕
Stone carving of double dragon
双竜の石彫り

蟹状缆船石
Crab – shaped mooring stone
蟹形の石の船杭

如意状缆船石
"Ruyi" – shaped mooring stone
如意形の石の船杭

花结状缆船石
Knot – shaped mooring stone
花形の石の船杭

人文荟萃

周庄,环境清静优雅,是读书的好地方,也颇有读书的好传统。历史上曾出过进士、举人20多位,除张翰、周迪功郎和明代江南巨富沈万三外,在近现代,还有不少知名人士寓居周庄,并留下不少翰墨华章。著名的人物有:张翰(张季鹰)、沈万三、徐民望、章腾龙、陶煦、陶焘、诸福坤、费毓卿、王大觉、叶楚伧、费公直、陶冷月、沈体兰等。

叶楚伧和他的故居　叶楚伧(1887－1946年),周庄人,同盟会会员,著名南社诗人,政治活动家。少年好学,兴新学后,考入苏州高等学堂。每年寒假从苏州回到周庄,看到不少人以赌为乐,吸食鸦片,败坏社会风气,便组织一批有志青年宣传赌博、迷信和吸食鸦片的危害,以此破旧习,创新风。辛亥革命爆发后,叶楚伧立即投笔从戎,加入粤军,任参谋长,随军北上,后又致力于宣传工作,创办《民立报》,即后来的《民国日报》。他主持《民国日报》,经费不足,向友人借贷,应付出版,维持10多年。著有《世徽堂诗稿》、《楚伧文存》及小说《古戍寒笳记》、《金阊之三月记》等作品。故居祖荫堂,位于西湾街,坐南朝北,前后五进,建于清同治年间。前堂楼为叶楚伧童年书房,后堂楼下客厅,叶曾在此与南社友人柳亚子、苏曼殊等斗酒叙诗,切磋艺文。庭院内花木扶疏,错落有致,春夏季节,满园鲜花盛开。

迷楼　位于贞丰桥畔,原名德记酒店。早在20年代初,南社发起人柳亚子、陈去病、王大觉,费公直等人四次在迷楼痛饮醋歌,乘兴赋诗,慷慨吟唱,后将百余首诗篇结为《迷楼集》流传于世。因此,周庄迷楼名声大振。现经修葺的迷楼仍保持当年风貌,依水傍桥,令人着迷。

Cultural Relics

Some famous ancient scholars were born or lived in Zhouzhuang. Besides Zhang Han, Zhou Digong and Shen Wansan, Xu Minwang, Zhang Tenglong, Tao Xu, Tao Tao, Chu Fukun, Fei Yuqing, Wang Dajue, Ye Chucang, Fei Gongzhi, Tao Lengyue and Shen Tilan all resided in Zhouzhuang in modern history.

Ye Chucang and His Former Residence
Ye Chucang (1887－1946), born in Zhouzhuang, was a poet of the South Society and a statesman, and was graduated from Suzhou High School. When he came home during winter vocation, he saw many people involving in gambling and opium, so he organized a group of young people to

publicize the harm of these activities. When the 1911 Revolution began, he joined the army. Then he established *Minli Daily* (later called *Minmeng Daily*), and also headed the *Minguo Daily* for more than 10 years. His works included *Poems of Shihui Hall*, *Collected Works of Chucang*, and some fictions.

His residence, Zuyin Hall, located on Xiwan Street facing north, was built in the Qing Dynasty, consisting of five courtyards. The Main Hall is a studio and the Rear Hall is a place where Ye received friends.

Milou Tower　　Milou Tower, once called De's Wineshop, is located at Zhenfeng Bridge. In the 1920s, the founders of the South Society, including Liu Yazi, Chen Qubing, Wang Dajue and Fei Gongzhi, went there four times to drink and compose poems. They published *Collected Works on Milou Tower* of more than 100 poems. Now, it has been rebuilt but retains its old style.

人物が輩出

　周荘は環境が静かで、本を読む雰囲気がただよい、昔から学問にいそしむ伝統がある。歴史上、進士、挙人（郷試に合格し、進士の試験を受ける資格を持った者）が20余人生まれ、張翰、周迪功郎、明代の江南の大富豪沈万三のほかに、近現代でも、多くの名士が周荘に住み、優れた文章や書画をたくさん残した。有名な人物に張翰（張季鷹）、沈万三、徐明望、章騰龍、陶煦、陶蕩、褚福坤、費毓卿、王大覚、葉楚傖、費公直、陶冷月、沈体蘭らがいる。

　葉楚傖とその旧居　葉楚傖（1887～1946）は周荘出身で、同盟会の会員、著名な南社の詩人、政治活動家であった。幼いころから勉強を好み、新学が興ってから、蘇州高等学堂に入った。毎年冬休みに蘇州から周荘に帰省し、賭博をしたり、阿片を吸飲したりする社会の悪習を見て、若い有志を組織して賭博、迷信、阿片吸飲の危害を宣伝し、古い悪習を打破し新しい気風を樹立するために活動した。辛亥革命が起こると、筆を投じて粤軍に入隊し、参謀長となり、軍隊とともに北上し、その後宣伝活動に力を注ぎ、『民国日報』の前身である『民立報』を創刊し、のちに『民国日報』を主宰し、経費が不足すると、友人から借り、出版を続け、10余年維持した。著作に『世徽堂詩稿』、『楚傖文存』および小説『古戍寒笳記』、『金閶之三月記』などがある。旧居の祖蔭堂は西湾街にあり、北向きで五つの庭があり、清の同治年間に建てた。前堂楼は葉楚傖の少年時代の書房で、後堂楼の一階は応接間で、葉楚傖はここで南社の友人であった柳亜子、蘇曼殊らと酒を飲みながら詩を語り、芸術と文学を互いに磨き合った。庭には木が茂り、春・夏になると、美しい花が咲きほこる。

　迷楼　貞豊橋の傍にあり、原名は徳記酒店といった。1920年代初期に、南社の発起人である柳亜子、陳去病、王大覚、費公直らがここで4回酒を痛飲し、歌を歌い、詩を作り、吟詠した。のちに100余首の詩が『迷楼集』に収録された。こうしたことから、周荘の迷楼は有名になった。修復された迷楼は当時の様子を保っている。

叶楚伧故居"祖荫堂"
Zuyin Hall of Ye Chucang's
Former House
葉楚傖旧居の「祖蔭堂」

三毛茶楼
Sanmao Teahouse
三毛茶楼

茶楼一角
A scene of teahouse
茶楼の一角

庭院幽深　　　　　戴氏老宅
A quiet courtyard　　Dai's House
幽静な庭　　　　　　戴氏の邸宅

迷楼
Milou Tower
迷楼

青糰
Polished glotinous rice balls
团子

周庄风味

素有"水乡泽国"之称的周庄,土地肥沃,物产丰饶;风味小吃,独具特色。

沈万三家宴:沈万三迁居周庄致富后,入乡随俗,热情待客,广邀地方名厨,选用水乡时鲜,精心配料,烹成各式风味独特的菜肴:万三蹄、清蒸鳜鱼、莼菜鲈鱼羹、姜汁田螺、塞肉油卜、百页包肉、双味豆干、焐熟河藕、三味圆等,冠以"万三家宴",流传至今。

万三蹄:为周庄首选名菜,以精选的猪后腿为原料,配以佐料,经过煨煮或蒸焖而成。肉质酥烂脱骨,汤色酱红,肥而不腻,咸甜相宜,香酥味美,十分可口。原为周庄过年、宴庆中主菜,意为团圆,后变为招待贵宾的上乘菜肴,传为沈万三家中待客必备的菜肴。

三味圆:用水面筋作皮,馅心以鸡脯肉、鲜虾仁、猪腿肉、葱、姜剁细,加黄酒等调料精制成圆,在鸡汤内煮熟。皮薄馅嫩,晶莹剔透,集点心、菜肴、鲜汤于一盆,鲜美至极,有口皆碑。

莼菜鲈鱼羹:鲈鱼有四鳃、两鳃之别。周庄鲈鱼为两鳃,体型略长,有鳜鱼似的花斑,但背上没有刺戟,肉质白嫩鲜美,无芒刺,历来为人称道。吃法很多,可红烧,可煮羹。煮羹时,配上莼菜,即莼菜鲈鱼羹,为菜肴之上品。西晋文学家张翰的"莼鲈之思",就是指他远在洛阳城,仍日夜思念家乡的这种美味。

白蚬汤:白蚬为贝类水鲜,产于蚬江。"稻熟螺蛳麦熟蚬",每年农历四月为白蚬上市季节。将蚬子洗净煮沸,放进调料,乳白色蚬子汤鲜美可口,营养丰富。可把蚬子肉挑出来炒菜,也很可口。

万三糕:已有数百年历史。镇上邹氏家族继承祖业,生产各式糕点,因用料讲究,品种众多,片薄滑糯,入口即化,深受欢迎。逢年过节,沈万三家常订购大批糕点赠送和招待亲朋,后被传作"万三糕",邹氏作坊随之也就有名了。

腌菜苋:每年暮春,当油菜抽薹时,人们摘下孕花的嫩薹,用清水洗净,放在阳光下晒成半干,然后装入小甏腌制。甏口用箬叶和黄泥密封,并倒置在

陶盆内,防止漏气。数月后将黄泥和箬叶去除,取出腌成的菜苋,一股清香扑鼻。既可生食,也可烧汤、炒菜。

Zhouzhuang's Delicious Food

Zhouzhuang enjoys rich natural resources and local specialties.

Family Feast of Shen Wansan When the rich man Shen Wansan moved to Zhouzhuang, he invited famous chefs, selected fresh aquatic products to create a series of delicacies after seasoning and cooking, such as Wansan Pig's Upper Leg, Streamed Mandarin Fish, Pottage of Vegetables and Perch, Ginger Sauce River Snail, Bean Curd Leaf Rolls with Minced Pork, Dried Double-Flavor Beancurd, Braised Lotus Root, and Three-Flavor Meatballs. These dishes have been handed down for generations.

Wansan Pig's Upper Leg This is Zhouzhuang's most famous delicacy. The pig's upper leg with flavorings is cooked or steamed until well-done. The soup, which turns red, is saline and sweet.

Three-Flavor Meatballs Chicken meat, fresh prawns, pork, shallots and ginger, as well as rice wine are packed inside gluten, and then made into round balls. They are boiled in chicken soup until well-done. It looks crystal-clear and very delicious.

Pottage of Vegetables and Perch Zhouzhuang's perch has two gills, and its nice meat can be cooked in many different ways. Boiling the perch with vegetables is one of the best ways to serve.

White Shellfish White shellfish are produced in Xianjiang River in April. They are washed first and boiled with some flavorings until well-done. The soup, which has a milky appearance, is richly nutritious. The meat can also be stir fried.

Wansan Cake This has a history of hundreds of years. The Zou's family used to produce various cakes for generations. This therapy is based on fine materials and offers many different kinds, which is welcomed by local people. Every holiday, Shen Wansan's family often ordered lots of cakes to give relatives and friends, thus creating the name of Wansan Cake.

Pickled Vegetables People collect fresh rape in late spring, then dry it in the sun. Before being completely dried out, however, they are put into an earthen jar, then sealed and put into an air-tight storage space. Several months later, the rape can be taken out and eaten directly, or used for cooking and in soup.

周荘の風味

「水郷沢国」といわれる周荘は土地が肥え、物産が豊富で、料理は独自の風味を持っている。

沈万三家宴 沈万三は周荘に移ってから財をなし、

郷に入っては郷に従い、心込めて客をもてなし、地方の名コックを広く招聘し、水郷の新鮮な材料を選んで、念入り調理させ、風味の独特な料理を作らせた。例えば万三家の豚肉料理、ケツギョ蒸し、ジュンサイとスズキのあつもの、タニシの生姜汁、肉をはさんだダイコンの油揚げ、豆腐で包んだ肉、双味の燻製豆腐、レンコン煮、三味だんごなどは「万三家宴」の料理として、今でも伝わっている。

　万三家の豚肉料理　周荘の名物料理で、精選したブタの後足を原料とし、調味料を入れ、とろ火で煮るか蒸したもので、肉が柔らかく、汁が醤油色を呈し、油っこくなく、塩の味と甘味が合って、口当たりがよい。もとは周荘の春節（旧正月）祝宴のメーン料理であったが、のちに客をもてなす上等の料理となり、沈万三家が賓客を招待する時に必ず出した料理である。

　三味だんご　麩素で皮を作り、鶏の胸肉、新鮮なエビのむき身、ブタの足肉、ネギ、千切りの生姜を黄酒などの調味料でよく混ぜって皮に包み、鶏肉スープで煮る。皮が薄くあんが柔らかく、透明で、大変美味しい。

　ジュンサイとスズキのあつもの　スズキには四えらと二えらの区別がある。周荘のスズキは二えらで、体がやや長く、ケツギョのような斑点があるが、背びれがあり、肉質が白くて柔らかくて、とげがなく、美味である。調理の方法も多く、醤油煮にもあつものにもできる。あつものを作る時には、ジュンサイを入れる。料理の上品である。西晋の文学者張翰の「莼鱸之思」は、彼が遠くの洛陽городで、古里のこのような美味を日夜思ったことを書いたものである。

　白蜆（シジミ）スープ　シジミは蜆江でとれる。「稲熟螺獅麦熟子蜆」、毎年の旧暦4月はシジミが市場に出

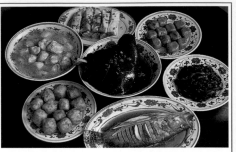

万三家宴
Wansan Family Feast
万三家料理

回る季節である。シジミをきれいに洗い、調味料を入れて煮る。乳白色のシジミ・スープは美味しく、栄養も豊富である。シジミの肉をとり出して炒めても、おいしい。

　万三カステラ　数百年の歴史をもっている。町の鄒氏の家族が祖業を受け継ぎ、いろいろなカステラを生産している。材料が厳選されたもので、種類も多く、厚さが薄く、口に入れると、すぐにとけ、人々から大変好まれている。祝祭日になると、沈万三家は数多くのカステラを注文して親戚や友人に贈ったりし、のちに万三カステラとして伝えられ、鄒氏の作業場もこれによって有名になった。

　塩漬け　毎年晩春、油菜の花茎が出るころ、花茎を摘みとり、水できれいに洗い、陽光で半干し、小さなかめに入れて塩漬けする。かめの口を若葉と黄色の泥で密封し、陶器の鉢の内に逆さに置き、空気がもれないようにする。数月後に、取り出す。香りがよく、スープや炒めものにもできる。

万三蹄
Wansan Pig's Upper Leg
万三家の豚肉料理
清蒸河鳗
Steamed river eel
田ウナギ蒸し

三味圆
Three‐Flavor Meatballs
三味だんご
清蒸鳜鱼
Streamed mandarin fish
ケイギョ蒸し

老宅门环
Old gate knocker
古い民家のドアノッカ

水乡风情

周庄,有悠久的历史和深厚的文化积淀,加上自然环境独特,形成纯朴的水乡民俗。

舞龙:在逢年过节和举办节庆活动时,都要舞龙。周庄的龙有黄龙和青龙,黄龙为男子汉们玩的,青龙为妇女们玩的。舞龙时配以舞狮,龙腾狮跃,栩栩如生。

划船:周庄有摇快船的习俗,此风始于清初。摇快船原是战争的需要。后来为庆祝丰收、节庆活动、婚嫁迎亲,也举办摇快船比赛。农民自备船只、服装、道具、锣鼓,自娱自乐,别具情趣。目前周庄有摇橹游船数十条,漫步河边,都会遇到游船在河中行驶。乘船游客在波光粼粼的水面上悠哉悠哉,看古镇风光,听船娘吴歌小唱,几多潇洒,几多风流。

阿婆茶:周庄人爱喝茶,而且吃茶的方式很讲究。茶具越古越好,煮水要用陶器瓦罐,燃料要用竹片树枝,沏茶要先点茶头,隔数分钟后,再用开水冲泡,这样可以保证茶的色、香、味。无论市镇和农村,人们经常看到六七十岁老太聚在一起吃茶,因此称为"阿婆茶"。现在周庄此风更盛。品茶时配以茶点:菜苋、瓜子、酥豆、各式蜜饯和点心。

Folklores of Water Township

Zhouzhuang enjoys rich cultural resources, a beautiful environment and simple local customs.

Dragon Dance: Men of Zhouzhuang always play the black dragon and women play the yellow dragon during holidays. Lion dance is also very common.

Fast Boating: This started in the Qing Dynasty. At first, it was the needs of war, then people held races for celebrating the harvest and holidays, also for weddings. Farmers participate with their own boats, clothes, props, gongs and drums. Zhouzhuang now has dozens of travel boats for tourists to do sightseeings around.

Grandmother Tea: People of Zhouzhuang are very fond of tea. They drink it in a tasteful way, using ancient tea sets, boiling water in pottery or earthen jars, bamboo slices or branches as fuel. They first wash the tea and then, several minutes later, pour on boiled water to guarantee the color, fragrance and taste.

People used to see groups of old women sitting together and drinking tea, and hence the name, grandmather tea. At present, people like to take some vegetables, melon seeds, beans and other pastries during the tea drinking.

水郷の風情

周荘は悠久な歴史と深い文化基盤があり、それに自然環境の独特さが加わり、純朴な水郷の風俗となっている。

竜の舞い　祝祭日や祝賀行事の時には、竜の舞いが披露される。周荘の竜は黄色と青色があり、黄色の竜は男子たち、青色の竜は女子たちがこれを持って踊る。獅子舞いと組合わせ、賑やかな雰囲気をかもし出す。

漕舟　周荘には清の初めから舟を漕ぐ風習がある。舟を漕ぐのはもともと戦争に必要であったからである。その後豊作、祝賀行事、嫁迎えの時に漕ぐようになり、レースも行われるようになった。農民は自ら舟、服装、道具、太鼓、銅鑼を用意し、自ら楽しむ。現在、周荘には櫓で漕ぐ観光舟が20余艘があり、川辺を歩いて見ると、川を行く観光舟をよく見かける。舟に乗って、古い町の風光を眺め、舟を漕ぐ娘の呉歌の民謡を聞くのも楽しい。

阿婆茶　周荘の人々はお茶をよく飲み、飲み方も非常に重視されている。茶具は古いほどよく、水を沸かすには陶器を使い、燃料は竹や枝を使い、まず少し茶をたて、数分間置いてから湯を入れる。こうすれば茶の色、香、味がよくなる。町でも農村でも、6、70歳のおばあさんが一緒に集まってお茶を飲んでいる光景をよく見かける。そのため、「阿婆茶」と言われる。周荘ではこの風潮が今でも残っている。お茶を飲む時、瓜の種、豆、いろいろな果肉の蜂蜜漬け、お菓子などが出される。

漫游水乡
Water township tour
水郷を歩く

水乡写生
Sketching the Water Township
水郷のスケッチ

梦里水乡
Water township
夢中の水郷

鱼鹰
Corm orant
カワウ

小桥流水人家
Bridge, water and house
小さな橋・川・民家

春绿江南
Spring Falls on Southern China
春の江南

捕鱼小舟
Fishing Boat
魚をとる小舟

周庄的春天
Spring at Zhouzhuang
周荘の春

'97中国苏州周庄国际旅游艺术节开幕式

艺术节
Art Festival
芸術祭

舞龙者
Dragon Dancer
竜を舞う人たち

挑花篮
Yangge Dance
花籠を担ぐ
(ヤンコ踊りの一種)

高蹺
Walk on stilts
高足踊り

周庄喜事多
Festival in Zhouzhuang
周荘のお祝い事

刺绣
Embroidering
刺繍

小酒家
Mini restaurant
小さなレストラン

阿婆茶
Grandmother tea
阿婆茶

丰收季节
Harvest season
豊作の季節

蒙蒙细雨
Drizzle
こぬか雨

油菜花香
Blooming rape
香が漂う油菜の花

淘米
Washing rice
米をとぐ

申江大酒店
Shenjiang Hotel
申江大酒店

Tourist Facilities

Shenjiang Hotel It is located at Jishui Port, and offers 100 standard rooms, six restaurants for 200 people, and a multi-function ball room.

Fengdan Double Bridge Holiday Resort It sits by the South Lake, and provides good marine food and entertainment facilities. It offers special motor and travel boats for private demand.

Yunhai Holiday Resort Situated to the south of the Grand Bridge, it consists of restaurants, guestrooms and various entertainment facilities, and is the best place for travelling and catering.

旅游设施

申江大酒店:位于周庄急水港畔,有标准房100间,大小餐厅6个,可容纳200多人同时就餐,还有多功能舞厅等其它设施。

枫丹双桥度假村:位于南湖畔,这里是集品尝河鲜、住宿、娱乐为一体的乡间度假休闲场所。度假村备有专用码头、快艇和游船,可以按宾客要求驶向江南水乡各地的旅游景点,实为久居闹市的人们养心休闲的世外桃园。

云海度假村:位于周庄大桥南堍,拥有餐厅、客房、网球场、溜冰场、游泳池、保龄球馆、桑拿中心、高速汽艇、游戏机房、桌球房等设施,是美食、娱乐、休闲为一体的度假胜地。

観光施設

申江大酒店(ホテル) 周荘の急水港のそばにあり、客室100室、200人余りが同時に食事することが収容できる大小のレストラン6軒、多用途のダンスホールなどの施設がある。

楓丹双橋リゾート村 南湖のほとりにあり、魚料理の賞味、宿泊、娯楽を一つにしたカントリー・リゾート村である。リゾート村には専用の船乗り場、ボート、観光舟が備えてある。賓客の希望により江南水郷の各地の観光名勝区をめぐることができ、都市に長く住んでいる人々に楽しめる場所を提供している。

雲海リゾート村 周荘大橋の南側にあり、レストラン、客室、テニスコート、スケート場、プール、ボーリング場、サウナセンター、モーターボート、ゲーム室、卓球室などの施設があり、グルメ、娯楽、レジャーを楽しめるリゾート区である。

云海度假村
Yunhai Holiday Resort
雲海リゾート

枫丹双桥度假村
Fengdan Double Bridge Holiday Resort
楓丹双橋リゾート

澄湖度假村
Chenghu Holiday Resort
澄湖リゾート

中房宾馆
Zhongfang Hotel
中房賓館

客房
Guest House
客室

文物商店
Antique Shop
文物商店

贞固堂
Zhengutang Guest House
貞固堂

宴会厅
Banquet Hall
宴会ホール

旺旺商店
Wangwang Store
旺旺商店

古色古乡
A local shopping lane
古びた商店街

旅游购物
Shopping
観光ショッピング

一游 二看 三尝
Watching and Tasting
見物・観賞・賞味